Outsourcing America

by Stephen Currie

ERICKSON PRESS

Yankton, South Dakota

ERICKSON PRESS

For more information, contact
Erickson Press
329 Broadway
PO Box 33
Yankton, SD 57078

Or you can visit our Internet site at www.ericksonpress.com.

Library of Congress Control Number: 2007920459
ISBN: 978-1-60217-008-7

Contents

Clintwood, Virginia

Clintwood is a small town in Virginia. The town is in the mountains. It is a beautiful town. But jobs are hard to find in Clintwood. Some people in the town work in stores. Some work in restaurants. Others work in coal mines. Most of these jobs do not pay much money. Still, these workers are lucky to have jobs. Many people who live there do not have jobs. One out of every ten adults in or near Clintwood cannot find work.

Finding a job in Clintwood was not always so hard. Many people there once worked for a big company. It was called Travelocity. They worked in a call center. People in call centers answer the phone when a customer calls. They make sales. They give out information. Travelocity gets lots of calls. So, it needs lots of workers. In 2004 about 275 people worked in the Clintwood call center.

The jobs at the call center did not pay a lot. Most workers made about $1300 a month. But that was not bad for the area. It was more pay

4

than these workers could get in other local jobs. And any job was better than no job. The call center helped the people of Clintwood earn a living.

Then in 2004 Travelocity closed the call center. The company did not go out of business. It moved the call center to India. The reason for the change was money. The company could pay Indian workers much less than it paid Americans. It would save money by closing the Clintwood call center.

The change helped the company. But it hurt Clintwood. All the call center workers lost their jobs. Many were not able to find new work. Some took jobs that paid less money. They found jobs

Travelocity outsourced this call center to India.

Some people who lost jobs in Clintwood became coal miners.

in stores and coal mines. A few had to drive 30 or 40 miles (48 or 64km) to find a new job. The loss of jobs was not good for Clintwood or for the people who lived there.

What happened in Clintwood has a name. It is called outsourcing. Jobs are outsourced when companies close offices and factories in the United States. Then they hire people to do the same jobs in other countries. Outsourcing is an important issue for today. It will also be an important issue in the future.

Jobs Leaving the Country

Outsourcing is fairly new. Hardly any American companies outsourced jobs until the 1980s. Factories and offices sometimes closed. A company sometimes went out of business. Or it shut down one workplace and opened a new one in another town or state. But companies almost never moved jobs to other countries.

There were reasons why outsourcing did not happen. The government charged extra money to bring goods into the United States. A few business leaders said that people outside the United States would not be good workers. Some said that other countries were not safe. They were afraid of wars and fights. They wanted to keep their workers and their property safe.

But the biggest problem was communication. It was hard to stay in touch with factories halfway across the world. Mail was slow. Phone calls cost lots of money. American business leaders had no good way to know what was going on in factories or offices overseas. So, they chose to keep most of their jobs at home.

Then came the 1980s and 1990s. Things began to change. Some new laws were passed. These laws made it easier to bring goods into the United States. Business leaders began to see that people in other lands could do good work. They saw that other countries were not so unsafe, after all.

Cities like Shanghai, China, welcome outsourced work.

Even more important, technology changed. Phone calls became cheaper. Mail became faster. And then came the Internet. The Internet made sending messages easy. A business owner in New York could keep in close touch with a factory in China. Distance was not the problem that it once had been.

Companies and Outsourcing

Manufacturers are companies that make goods. Most of them make these goods in factories. They were the first businesses to outsource. They started outsourcing in the 1980s. For instance, some car companies closed factories in Michigan and other states. The workers lost their jobs. Then the companies opened new factories in Mexico. They hired Mexican workers to build their cars.

Other manufacturers soon did the same. The Levi Strauss company makes jeans. It shut down factories all over the United States. Then it opened new factories in Mexico. Thousands of American workers lost their jobs. The Radio Flyer company makes toy wagons. It closed its factory in Chicago and fired about 90 people. Then it built a new factory in China. Another company had over 1,000 workers at a big factory in Massachusetts. These workers built computer parts. The company moved these jobs to Asia and Mexico. That put the Americans out of work.

Levi Strauss has moved factories abroad.

Where the Jobs Go

Jobs that are outsourced go to many different countries. India probably gets more of these jobs than any other country today. India has a stable government. It has many well-educated people. Many Indians are very poor and are eager to work. And lots of Indians speak English. These are all good reasons for companies to choose India.

But American jobs also move to other nations. China is getting more and more of these jobs. Thousands go to Mexico. Others go to Romania and Russia, Ghana and South Africa, Argentina and Vietnam. U.S. jobs are being outsourced all over the world.

At first it seemed that only factory jobs were at risk. But that changed in the late 1990s. Other kinds of jobs started leaving the country, too. Soon many types of jobs were being outsourced. By the early 2000s most outsourced jobs were not in factories. "It's the high tech, high end, high paying jobs that are heading out of town,"[1] one expert told Congress.

These changes have hit workers in many kinds of businesses. Hundreds of call center jobs have moved to India. Some banks are closing offices in the United States. They are training new workers in other countries. Thousands of computer jobs have been outsourced. Some have gone to India. Some have gone to China. Some are heading for other nations. But they are leaving the United States.

Jobs like nursing cannot be outsourced.

Some jobs cannot be outsourced. Nurses need to see and touch their patients. Police officers must watch American streets. The United States will always have jobs for plumbers and cooks. Still, workers outside the United States can do many other kinds of jobs. For now, Americans still hold most of these jobs. But that may not always be true. One expert says that one in every ten American jobs could be outsourced someday.

Numbers of Jobs

No one knows for sure how many jobs have left the United States because of outsourcing. Businesses do not have to report how many jobs they outsource. The government does not count factories that close. It does not count jobs that leave. The only way to know is to make a guess, which is called an estimate.

Outsourcing or Not?

Many companies do not like to admit that they are outsourcing. They think that many Americans will be angry at them. People who are angry may stop buying their products. Then the companies will lose money. So, some companies try very hard to say they are not outsourcing.

In 2004, for instance, a phone company closed an office in Massachusetts. Then the company opened new offices abroad. Some workers in these offices were doing jobs that the workers in Massachusetts had done. The workers said that their jobs had been outsourced. Most observers agreed.

But company officials did not agree. They said that they were not outsourcing. They said that the jobs were no longer needed. The company had new ideas. So it was working on other things. The company leaders said that the new offices had nothing to do with the closing of the one in Massachusetts. In their minds, they did not outsource.

How Many U.S. Jobs Are Outsourced?

No one knows for certain how many U.S. jobs are outsourced. Shown below are a few professions and estimates of the jobs outsourced from each in 2005.

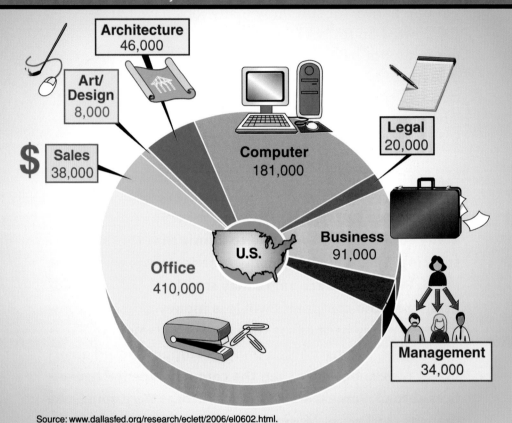

Architecture 46,000

Art/Design 8,000

Sales 38,000

Computer 181,000

Legal 20,000

Business 91,000

U.S.

Office 410,000

Management 34,000

Source: www.dallasfed.org/research/eclett/2006/el0602.html.

But guessing is not easy. And so, people's guesses are very different. Most experts say that companies move about 200,000 jobs each year. Many others say the number is more. Some say the total is closer to 300,000. Some argue that it is well over 400,000! And a few think it may be much, much less.

Finding an exact total is hard. But one thing is clear. Many companies are outsourcing. Many workers are losing their jobs. They say that their companies are moving work to China, India, and Mexico. One expert took a poll of over 100 companies in 2006. He asked if they were thinking about sending jobs overseas. More than half said that they were.

Money

Outsourcing makes good sense for many companies. The main reason is money. Most outsourced jobs go to Asia or Latin America. Workers in these

Moving call centers to India saves U.S. companies money.

places earn far less than workers in the United States. A company with many workers can save a lot of money by outsourcing. Call centers are a good example. Call center workers in Clintwood, Virginia, earned about $1300 a month. That is not much money in the United States. But $1300 a month is a fortune to a worker in India. Indian call center workers might make $1300 in a year. A company could hire ten or twelve Indian workers for the money they paid one American. Travelocity saved millions of dollars when it sent its call center jobs to India.

Saving money is important. It is so important that some companies say they must send jobs abroad. If they do not, they will go out of business. The W.C. Bradley company makes grills. In 2004 it moved 500 jobs from Georgia to China. Company leaders said they were sorry. But they also said they had to make a change. They said that their business was not making money. They could not raise prices. People might stop buying their grills. So, they had to cut wages. That meant outsourcing. "We really don't have any other choice if we want to continue in this business,"[2] one official said.

Other Advantages

Saving on labor costs is a big reason to outsource. But it is not the only one. Companies that outsource save money in other ways, too. Many countries want American companies to hire their

Where Do Outsourced Jobs Go?

Jobs from the United States are outsourced all over the world. Some of the main outsourcing locations appear here.

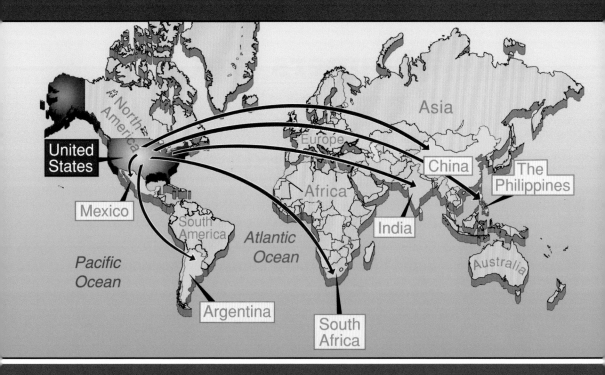

people. Some of these countries build factories and offices for companies that send jobs abroad. They give the buildings to the companies free of charge. Or they may not make these companies pay taxes.

Outsourcing also lets U.S. businesses sell more goods. Few people in countries like India or China have much money. So, they cannot buy many goods. U.S. jobs bring money to these countries. Then people can buy more goods. American companies make some of these goods. That brings in money. In this way, companies may make more money by sending jobs abroad.

Shoppers and Savings

Companies can do different things with the money they save. Some of them raise the pay of their leaders. Or they use the money to buy other companies. But they can also lower their prices. And many companies do just that. W.C. Bradley grills cost less now that its factory is overseas. Radio Flyer wagons cost less, too. Other compa-

Shoppers benefit when outsourcing companies save money.

nies also cut their prices when they go abroad. Or they do not raise their prices as quickly.

In this way, outsourcing does not just help American companies. It can help ordinary Americans, too. American shoppers save money when prices are lower. Outsourcing lets Americans buy cheaper grills, jeans, and toys. So, outsourcing lets ordinary American shoppers save money.

In some ways, then, outsourcing is good. It helps American businesses. It can be good for American consumers. Without outsourcing, some companies might close. Shoppers might have to pay much more for shoes or cars. For these reasons, many Americans think that outsourcing works. "It is a plus for the economy in the long run,"[3] says an adviser to President George W. Bush. For him and for many other Americans, the advantages of outsourcing are worth the cost.

Chapter 2

Problems for Workers

Outsourcing can help businesses. Sometimes it even helps shoppers. But outsourcing hurts people, too. People lose jobs when companies outsource. That can cause big problems. Many of these people struggle to find new jobs. Those who get work often make less money than before. So, outsourcing hurts workers who lose their jobs. And it can hurt American communities as well.

Losing a Job

It is always hard to lose a job. It is hard for workers when their companies go out of business. It is hard for workers when their companies move out of state. It is hard for workers when companies do not need their skills any more. Outsourcing is just one more way of losing a job. But some workers are especially angry when they lose their jobs to outsourcing.

For years the La-Z-Boy furniture company had three factories in Pennsylvania. Many workers had good jobs at the factories. But La-Z-Boy closed all three factories in 2004. It opened a new factory in China. A total of 425 La-Z-Boy workers lost their jobs. Some of these people had worked for the company for over 30 years. Many felt betrayed by the company.

Some laid-off workers go further. They feel that their country has betrayed them. Natasha Humphries had a good job with the Palm technology company. Then Palm outsourced her work to India. "I was raised to think that getting an education and working hard assures you a good and steady job,"[4] says Humphries. Now she says that she was wrong. She is angry at Palm. But she

La-Z-Boy furniture like this is now made in China.

Training Replacements

Stephen Gentry was a computer programmer in Washington. He worked for a company called Boeing. In 2003 Gentry learned that his job was moving to India. But first Gentry was told to train the workers who would be taking his job. The Indian workers came to Washington. They met with Gentry each day. He taught them what they needed to know. Then his job ended.

Gentry was shocked and hurt. He thought it was not right to have to train his replacements. Many other U.S. workers have had to train their replacements, too. Most of them agree that it is a terrible idea. Some even say it is the worst part of losing their jobs.

is also angry at the U.S. government. She thinks it must do more to keep jobs in the United States.

Fears and Outsourcing

Many workers who lose their jobs are afraid. A few people find a new job quickly and easily. Some of them find good jobs. They find jobs that they are trained to do. They find jobs that pay well. But they are the lucky ones. Most workers worry that they will not find a new job. Or they fear that they will have to work harder for less money. They do not see a bright future ahead.

These fears make sense for many displaced workers. Displaced workers are people who lose their jobs. Experts say that these workers will have trouble finding new jobs that pay well. About one-third of displaced workers may not find a full-time job again for many months or years. Another third will find new full-time work but for lower pay. Only about one-third of all displaced workers will ever earn the same wages again.

Anti-Outsourcing Laws

Some states have passed anti-outsourcing laws to protect American workers. Many others have proposed such laws.

Anti-outsourcing laws passed
Proposed anti-outsourcing laws
No anti-outsourcing laws

Source: National Foundation for American Policy/Federal Reserve Bank of Dallas. Data as of 2005.

The stories of individual workers show what can happen. Ruth Schumacher once made $11 an hour building bicycles in Ohio. Then the company outsourced her job to China. After that she worked part-time at a hotel. She made just $7 an hour. Mike Emmons was a computer programmer in Florida. His job was outsourced to India. Like Schumacher, he found a new job. But this job paid about half the money he once earned.

Some displaced workers cannot find new jobs that match their skills. Computer work is a good example. More and more computer jobs are leaving the country. Fewer companies are left to hire programmers who are out of work. The same is true for manufacturing. Once, most clothes sold in the United States were made in America. Today over 80 percent are made elsewhere. Little by little, these jobs have been outsourced. There are few jobs left for Americans who want to make clothing.

School and Retraining

Some displaced workers go back to school. Others go through job retraining. Job retraining programs teach them skills for new careers. Job retraining can work. Some programmers have become nurses. People who lost their jobs at call centers have become teachers. A few of these people earn more money than ever before. And others have jobs they know they will keep.

Some Americans who lose their jobs go back to school.

But these programs do not work for everyone. Petra Mata once worked for Levi Strauss. Then the company moved her job to Costa Rica. She tried to take high school classes for adults. Her goal was to get a diploma. That would help her find a better job. "But when I arrived," she says, "there was no teacher and no books."[5] Funding was low. The program could not help her.

There are other problems with retraining, too. Many training programs cost money. People without jobs may not be able to afford them. It can be hard to train older workers for new jobs. And some new careers may not be good choices. When factory workers lost their jobs in the 1980s, it made sense for them to learn to use computers. Today computer jobs are being outsourced, too.

Most displaced workers do not see good times ahead. They are angry, sad, and scared. They may feel that no one in government or business cares about them. Younger workers wonder if they will ever get a good job. Older workers wonder what they should do now. "I'm 54 years old," said one man whose job was moved to India, "and I'm virtually starting over."[6]

Communities

Outsourcing is a problem for workers who lose their jobs. But it can hurt whole towns, too. In many places, a large factory or office keeps the local economy going. This company hires many

Columbus, Indiana

Columbus, Indiana, is the home of a large company called Cummins Inc. Cummins makes engines and other goods. Many people in Columbus work at Cummins. But that number is fewer than it once was. Cummins has been outsourcing jobs to Mexico, India, and other countries. As a result, Cummins has fewer workers in Indiana than it used to.

That means fewer jobs for the people of Columbus. It also means jobs that do not pay as well. Factory jobs used to pay $20 an hour. People who found new jobs in stores only get $8 or $10 an hour. The average family in the area earns less money now than it did in 1995. Charities are helping more people. More children are getting free lunches at school.

Cummins is hoping to keep as many jobs in Columbus as it can. But it is hard to sell engines when other companies can sell them for less money. To stay in business, Cummins officials say their company must outsource. And that hurts the people of Columbus.

workers. These workers support nearby stores and businesses. They eat at local diners. They get their cars fixed at repair shops. They go to movie theaters. They buy books and toys. Small businesses need these customers to survive.

When a company moves its workforce to another place, local businesses suffer. People who do not have work eat out less. They may try to fix

Etch-a-Sketch toys are now made in China.

their cars themselves. They see fewer movies and buy fewer books. They cut back on spending. That hurts local businesses. Often stores and restaurants cannot stay open. "A lot of smaller businesses have closed since the Levi plant left town,"[7] reports a woman in Tennessee.

The closing of businesses is not the only problem. When jobs are hard to find, people move away. The value of houses drops. Fewer people pay taxes. Towns and cities may run low on money. They may offer fewer services. All these changes hurt a community. In 2003 the Etch-a-Sketch toy company shut down a factory in Bryan, Ohio. It moved 200 jobs to China. One observer said that the closing of the factory "seemed to take a piece of Bryan's heart."[8]

More Worries

Outsourcing can also affect people who still have jobs. Some workers worry that they will lose their jobs, too. Many call center workers feel that way. So do many computer programmers. So do other people who work in industries that already outsource. They expect that their jobs will not stay in America for long. "All engineering jobs will go overseas,"[9] predicts one worker from Minnesota.

Outsourcing may also force people to choose between jobs and high pay. Some companies say they might move their factories abroad. Then they ask workers to accept pay cuts. Workers are afraid that they will lose their jobs if they do not agree. So, they often accept the lower wages. They reason that less pay is better than no job at all. "Many garment workers who were paid one dollar for sewing a piece of clothing," says a California woman, "are now only making fifty cents for the same amount of work."[10]

Marchers express their views on outsourcing.

It is clear that outsourcing hurts many workers. It also can hurt communities. And if outsourcing becomes more common, more workers and communities will be hurt. It is important for business and government leaders to see the effects that outsourcing can have on people. There are good parts to outsourcing. But there are plenty of problems with it, too. If outsourcing lasts, people will need to try to fix those problems.

Workers Abroad

Outsourcing affects American workers in many ways. But outsourcing affects people in other countries as well. Foreign workers are taking jobs that have been outsourced. This has happened in countries such as India, Mexico, China, and Brazil. These new jobs have changed some towns and nations quite a bit. They have changed the way people live in other countries. What happens to these workers is important, too.

Life in Poor Nations

In many ways, outsourcing helps foreign workers. Companies usually outsource jobs to poor nations. These countries do not have jobs for all their people. Millions of people in these nations are unemployed. Many of them have never had jobs. They may live in tents or shacks. They may have to beg for food in the streets.

Sometimes life is not much better for people who do have jobs. Many workers have little education. They have few job skills. Most earn very low wages. A worker in a store or a factory might earn less than a dollar a day. Prices are lower than they are in the United States. Still, these workers can barely afford basic food and shelter.

Even skilled workers may struggle in these nations. India is a good example. India has many computer programmers. It has more engineers than the United States. These people have college degrees. They are eager to work. But the Indian economy is not strong. It does not produce enough jobs for all of these men and women. Many of these workers cannot find jobs that use their skills. They need jobs outsourced by foreign companies.

Wages and Change

The outsourcing of jobs can make life easier for people in nations such as India and Mexico. U.S. businesses build new offices and factories in these countries. They teach people new skills. They help workers use the skills they already have. They buy supplies from nearby businesses. All of these changes can help towns and communities.

U.S. companies build offices and factories in other countries.

And these changes do take place. During the 1990s, Internet provider AOL moved some jobs to the Philippines. AOL paid its new workers $5.50 a day. That may not sound like much. It is not much by U.S. standards. But it was much more than most local companies paid their workers. AOL is not the only company like this. Some other U.S. companies also pay their workers more than local businesses do.

This helps workers at these companies. It can also help people who live nearby. These people know that the U.S. companies pay better wages. That can force local businesses to pay more. If the businesses do not, their workers might leave. They may choose to work for the higher-paying American firm instead.

In India these changes are easy to see. Indian computer programmers made a lot more money in 2003 than they made in 2002. Some of these people worked for U.S. companies. Others worked for Indian companies. Programmers still earn less in India than they do in the United States. But the gap is closing.

New Jobs and Opportunities

Outsourcing can help foreign workers in other ways, too. By adding jobs, it reduces unemployment. It also helps some workers get better jobs. This can be seen in places like Bangalore, India.

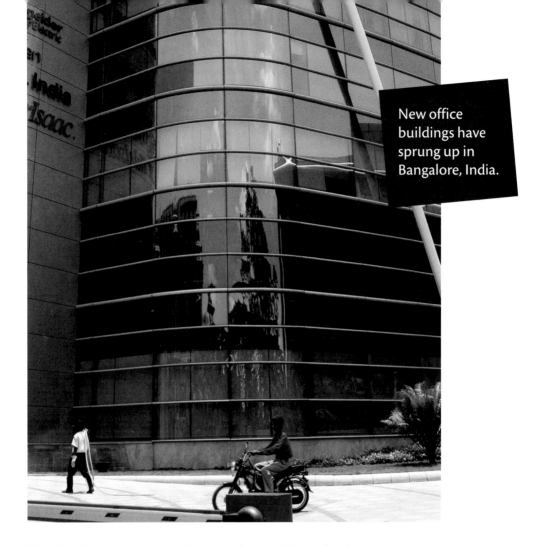

New office buildings have sprung up in Bangalore, India.

Technology companies such as Google have moved jobs to Bangalore. The city once did not have much work for its people. Now Bangalore is a center for technical jobs.

New jobs can also teach foreign workers new skills. Author Thomas Friedman is pleased that AOL hired so many workers in the Philippines. Friedman thinks the work will help Filipinos learn more about technology. It will give them new opportunities. "You can bet the smartest ones will soon go off and start their own little tech

The Fair Labor Association

The Fair Labor Association is a U.S. group that started in the 1990s. This group tries to make sure that companies treat their foreign workers fairly. The Fair Labor Association tells companies not to hire children, for instance. And it reminds companies to give their workers time off.

The Fair Labor Association works hard. Many U.S. companies are part of the association. They promise to follow the group's rules. These companies usually do treat their workers fairly.

But other American companies ignore the rules. They hire children. They make their workers spend too many hours on the job. The Fair Labor Association is not a police force. It cannot make companies follow the rules. Some people say that the Fair Labor Association is not enough. They say that the United States needs laws that force companies to treat their workers right.

companies,"[11] Friedman writes. If they do, that will be good for the workers. It will also be good for the Philippines.

Poor Treatment

Still, outsourcing is not always good for foreign workers. Some American companies mistreat the workers they hire. In 2005 an American named Jane Galvin taught English to call center workers in India. Her students told her that they took calls ten hours a day. Then they had to go to meetings. These meetings lasted two hours more. The workers got one fifteen-minute break all day.

Many call center workers quit after a few months. They could not handle the poor working conditions. But the company would not change its rules. Galvin points out that company leaders did not need to make changes. Jobs were hard to find in India. It was easy for the company to find new workers. "I hope that working conditions . . . improve in time," Galvin says, "but I am unsure."[12]

These call center workers were not treated well. Still, they were treated better than many

Honduran factory workers make less than $30 a week.

Shenzhen

The city of Shenzhen is in China. In 1980 it was a small place with little wealth. Some of its money came from trade. Ships sometimes came near the town. They traded goods with local merchants. But much of Shenzhen's money came from fishing.

Then the leaders of China decided to make Shenzhen a place for business. Since 1980 it has grown in people and in wealth. Today Shenzhen is a center for outsourcing. Many American companies have moved offices to Shenzhen. Many engineers and programmers live and work there. The new jobs have brought pollution to Shenzhen. And it is hard to find places for all the new people to live. But new business has mostly been good to Shenzhen and its people.

other foreign workers. Some factory workers tell of being locked inside their workplaces all day. Others complain of long hours. One U.S. factory in China almost never gave its workers a day off. The workers spent fourteen hours a day on the job.

More Problems

Factory workers are also under lots of pressure to do their work. Lydda Gonzalez made shirts in a factory in Honduras. Her work crew had to finish more than 2,000 shirts each day. That was almost impossible. But the bosses pushed the crew to work faster and faster. That made Gonzalez feel like a machine, not a person. "It is forbidden to talk," she said. "You can't move or stretch, or even look to the side."[13]

Working in these factories can be unsafe, too. Many foreign countries do not check factories to make sure they are safe. When workers are tired, machinery may hurt them. When they are working too fast, they may injure themselves. Or they may become sick from overwork. In one factory, workers had no time to eat lunch. Late in the day, some fainted from hunger.

Pay is a problem, too. Some U.S. companies pay very low wages. In 1998 Kmart factories paid

African textile workers fill orders for Wal-mart and the Gap.

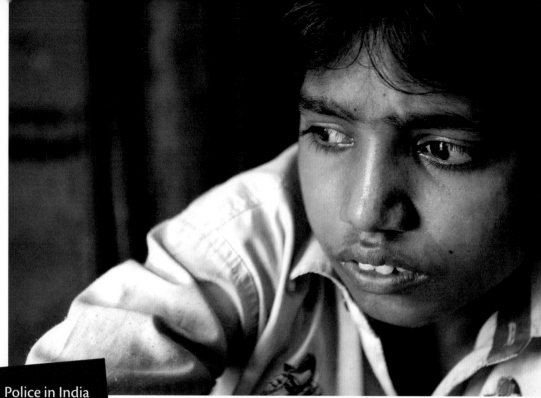

Police in India rescued this young worker from a factory.

their foreign workers around 28 cents an hour. Workers at some Wal-mart factories made even less. These low wages have made many people angry. They have complained to the companies. Kmart and Wal-mart have raised some of their pay rates a little. But the wages are still low. The same is true of many other American businesses.

U.S. companies often make rules to help their foreign workers. Some say that these workers can be on the job just eight or ten hours a day. Some make sure the workers get plenty of breaks. Some say they will not hire children. But companies do not always follow their own rules. One example was ACCO. This company made staplers and paper clips. It said it did not hire people under eighteen. But it hired a Mexican worker named Maria Hernandez when she was just fifteen. "When they need people, they don't ask many questions,"[14] Hernandez told a reporter.

Fixing the Problems

Leaders of U.S. companies know there are some problems with outsourcing. They say that most companies treat their workers well. They also argue that U.S. companies are not always to blame for problems. Sometimes the companies do not know what is going on. Managers in India or China sometimes break the rules. Then the managers hide the truth from the company. It can take time for officials to learn what is really happening.

These company leaders are partly right. However, some American companies do keep close track of their factories abroad. They make phone calls. They expect to see reports and e-mails. They listen to complaints from workers. They make sure their own rules are followed. They fire managers who treat workers badly. It would be good if all U.S. companies did the same.

Chapter 4

Getting Creative

Outsourcing is a hot topic today. It will still be a hot topic for the near future. Most people agree that outsourcing will be around for a few more years. Many think it will be around for a lot longer. One expert says that 50 million jobs could be sent abroad! But others disagree. They think that the real number will be far fewer.

But these are only guesses. No one knows if outsourcing will rise or fall as time goes on. In part, businesses will decide. Companies want to keep doing things that make money. If outsourcing helps companies make money, it will continue. But what if outsourcing stops bringing in money? Then companies will stop outsourcing. They will try to make money in other ways.

Second Thoughts

This change is already happening. A few American companies are wondering if outsourcing is best for them. In 2006 a business group talked to some companies that sent jobs abroad. About one company in ten said it planned to do less outsourcing in the future. Some were not saving very much money. They had hoped they would save more. Others did not like the quality of the work. Still others found that it was hard to keep in touch with workplaces abroad.

And some companies are choosing not to outsource at all. A good example is Frontier Airlines.

Outsourcing continues to be a hot topic.

Frontier Airlines does not outsource its call centers.

Frontier had a chance to outsource its call centers. But it decided not to. Company leaders say that their call center workers do a great job. They are helpful and friendly. If Frontier outsourced these jobs, the customers might be upset. Then they might stop flying on Frontier's planes. In this way, outsourcing could hurt ticket sales. So, Frontier officials think it is better to keep the jobs in the United States.

Laws and Public Opinion

Frontier's decision pleases many Americans who do not like outsourcing. These people want other companies to make the same choices. They hope that companies will decide not to outsource so much.

Still, some of these Americans are not willing to wait. They do not want to sit back and see what happens. They want to make changes now. They hope to make it harder to make money by outsourcing. That will make outsourcing less common.

Some of these people hope to pass new laws. They think the government should play a role. They think it should try to keep companies from sending jobs abroad. It can force companies to pay higher taxes if they move jobs overseas. And the government can stop doing business with companies that outsource.

Why Not Ban Outsourcing?

Outsourcing causes some big problems. Some people wonder why the U.S. government does not ban it. The U.S. government has the power to make outsourcing illegal. But that will probably not happen soon. The United States tries not to tell companies what to do. Americans think it is good when companies make decisions for themselves. Also, a law like this could be very hard to enforce. A company might close a factory in the United States. Then it might wait a year before opening a new one overseas. That way it would look like it was not outsourcing. So, most Americans do not support a law that would ban outsourcing.

Outsourcing angers these American flight attendants.

People who oppose outsourcing have another plan, too. This plan is to change the way people think. They hope to make people angry about outsourcing. So, they talk about what happens when jobs leave America. They tell their friends to buy goods that are made in the United States. "As long as Radio Flyers [toy wagons] are made in China," says one writer, "I'll never buy another one."[15]

These ideas could work. Companies do not want to pay more taxes. They do not want people to stop buying their products. They do not want the government to stop working with them. These things will cost them money. Perhaps these companies will lose lots of money. Then they may decide that outsourcing is not a good plan.

New Ideas

Other people who are against outsourcing have a different idea. They do not want to tell companies what to do. They are not sure that they can stop all outsourcing. But they want to make it easier for companies to stay in the United States. That means being creative. It means helping companies find good workers. It means training workers to do jobs that are needed. And it means asking companies to think about more than just money. That will take lots of new ideas.

At job fairs, employers can find skilled workers like this man.

One idea has to do with matching workers to
companies that need them. Ron and Anil Hira are
writers. They know a lot about outsourcing. "We
have heard from many employers who say they
cannot find the right workers," they write. "At the
same time, we have heard from thousands of high-
ly qualified workers who cannot find a job."[16]
Some of these companies say they have to outsource because it is so hard to find good people. So,
one way to keep companies in the United States is
to match them with good American workers.

The Hiras think that job retraining can help meet this goal. They say that the United States must spend more money on retraining. It is not good for anyone when displaced workers cannot find new jobs. It hurts the workers. It hurts their communities. The Hiras think that it hurts the whole nation. They argue that it is better to put lots of money into retraining programs. This would help the workers. It would also make sure that Americans have skills that companies need.

But the Hiras also say that money is not enough. They think the United States must change the way it runs these programs. "We are in a new era of work and lifelong learning,"[17] the Hiras write. So, retraining has to be flexible. It must give people many kinds of skills. It must help people hold more than one kind of job. That is good for workers and the companies. It is good for the economy. And it is good for the whole nation.

New Ideas for Companies

Many people also hope to change how U.S. companies act. They want company leaders to think in new ways. Right now, many companies think about next year or the year after. They do not think about ten or twenty years from now. But what is best for a company today may not be best in ten years. For instance, it is good for businesses if U.S. workers have jobs that pay well. "If American

Outsourcing to Minnesota

Dave La Reau is a computer programmer. He used to live in Chicago. Then his job was outsourced. For a while he had no job at all. Then he got a job offer from a company called CrossUSA. CrossUSA wanted La Reau to work with computers.

But CrossUSA did not want La Reau to stay in Chicago. They sent him to Sebeka, Minnesota. Chicago is a big place. Sebeka is very small. Only about 700 people live there. Sebeka is also a long way from big stores or museums. And La Reau did not earn as much money as he earned in Chicago.

Still, it was a good move for La Reau. Sebeka is a quiet place to live. Land is cheap in Sebeka. Houses are cheap, too. So La Reau did not need as much money as he did before. La Reau is one of many workers whose jobs are being outsourced to rural America.

workers are unemployed," Ron and Anil Hira ask, "who will buy their products?"[18]

Companies also can work more closely with schools. That is especially true for colleges and high schools. They can let schools know what kinds of jobs they are offering now. They can also describe jobs they think they will need in the future. Teachers can help train young workers in these areas. Then these new workers have jobs that will stay in the United States. And the companies have good workers to hire. This is good for companies. And it is good for workers, too.

Outsourcing to America

One other idea involves rural America. Some people think that companies should move jobs to rural America. Then they would not send jobs to India or Mexico. Rural land is cheap. Wages are low. So, businesses can save money. They can

Protesters display "pink slips," which are a symbol of being fired.

CrossUSA's boss (right) moved one of his offices to rural North Dakota.

keep jobs in the United States. And they can easily keep in touch with rural workplaces.

There are other reasons to move to rural areas, too. Many small towns and villages have good roads. Some have airports nearby. Most have high-speed Internet and good phone service. Almost all of them have room to build new offices and factories. These rural parts of the United States have good workers with good educations, too.

And rural people would welcome companies that move in. Most rural areas do not offer many jobs. One business leader calls outsourcing "rural America's next big opportunity."[19] Some companies have already done this. It has happened in Sebeka, Minnesota. It has also happened in Magnolia, Arkansas. Other companies are doing the same.

Solving the Problems

There are some big problems with outsourcing. But Americans are very creative. Many Americans are working to solve these problems. They hope to keep the United States strong and rich. They want workers to have jobs that pay well. They

A college student takes part in a job fair.

Knock your career out of the ball park

want workers to enjoy their jobs. And they want these jobs to be secure.

These Americans have many good ideas about outsourcing. Perhaps they will stop it forever. More likely, they will not. But even if they do not, their ideas can help. These people want to make outsourcing less painful. They want to solve some of the problems that outsourcing can cause. They want to change the way people think about jobs. It is good to know that many creative people are trying to solve these problems.

Notes

Chapter 1: Jobs Leaving the Country

1. Quoted in United States Senate Committee on the Judiciary, "Testimony of Mr. Michael Gildea," July 29, 2003. http://judiciary.senate.gov/testimony.cfm?id=878&wit_id=2517.
2. Quoted in Peralte C. Paul, "Grill Maker to Close Plant," *Atlanta Journal-Constitution*, November 18, 2004, p. E3+.
3. Quoted in Douglas Kiker, "Bush Econ Advisor: Outsourcing OK," CBS News, February 13, 2004. www.cbsnews.com/stories/2004/02/13/opinion/main600351.shtml.

Chapter 2: Problems for Workers

4. Quoted in Show Us the Jobs, "Natasha: Santa Clara, California." www.showusthejobs.com/51stories/ca.cfm.
5. Quoted in Christine Ahn, ed., *Shafted*. Oakland, CA: Food First, 2003, p. 33.
6. Quoted in Kathy Kiely, "As Jobs Go Overseas, a City Struggles to Reinvent Itself," *USA*

Today, March 21, 2004. www.usatoday.com/news/nation/2004-03-21-outsourcing-usat_x.htm.

7. Quoted in Show Us the Jobs, "Shirley: Powell, Tennessee." www.showusthejobs.com/51stories/tn.cfm.

8. Byron L. Dorgan, *Take This Job and Ship It.* New York: St. Martin's, 2006, p. 29.

9. Quoted in Ron Hira and Anil Hira, *Outsourcing America.* New York: Amacom, 2005, p. 130.

10. Quoted in Ahn, *Shafted,* p. 37.

Chapter 3: Workers Abroad

11. Thomas Friedman, *The Lexus and the Olive Tree.* New York: Anchor, 2000, p. 52.

12. Jane E. Galvin, "Inside an Indian Call Center: The Big Disconnect," *Christian Science Monitor*, June 23, 2006, p. 9+.

13. Quoted in Dorgan, *Take This Job and Ship It*, p. 57.

14. Quoted in John R. MacArthur, *The Selling of "Free Trade."* New York: Hill and Wang, 2000, p. 348.

Chapter 4: Getting Creative

15. Quoted in Dorgan, *Take This Job and Ship It*, p. 38.

16. Hira and Hira, *Outsourcing America*, p. 183.
17. Hira and Hira, *Outsourcing America*, p. 182.
18. Hira and Hira, *Outsourcing America*, p. 197.
19. Dale King, "Outsourcing: Rural America's Next Big Opportunity." http://cbdd.typepad.com/rural/2004/08/outsourcing_rur.html.

Glossary

abroad: Having to do with other countries.

call center: An office where people answer phone calls for a company.

displaced worker: A person who has lost a job.

economy: The way people use goods and services.

garment worker: A person who makes clothing.

manufacture: To build things in factories.

outsourcing: Sending jobs to other countries.

profit: Money that is made by companies.

technology: The use of new ideas to make tools and machines.

unemployed: Not having a job.

wages: Money paid to workers.

Bibliography

Books

Christine Ahn, ed., *Shafted*. Oakland, CA: Food First, 2003. A short book about the effects of U.S. economic policy on workers. The book includes some firsthand accounts from people whose jobs were outsourced.

Adrian Cooper, *Fair Trade? A Look at the Way the World Is Today*. Mankato, MN: Stargazer, 2006. A discussion of fair trade and other economic issues in the world. Fair trade is closely connected to outsourcing.

Katherine Read Dunbar, *At Issue: Does Outsourcing Harm America?* San Diego: Greenhaven, 2006. An in-depth look at the issues. A higher reading level than most of these other books.

Brendan January, *Globalize It!* Brookfield, CT: Twenty-First Century, 2003. Describes issues in globalization and the building of a global economy. Some of these issues overlap with outsourcing.

Terence O'Hara, *The Economy*. Philadelphia: Chelsea House, 2001. A basic guide to economics, jobs, and business.

Periodicals

Jane E. Galvin, "Inside an Indian Call Center: The Big Disconnect," *Christian Science Monitor*, June 23, 2006.

Kathy Kiely, "As Jobs Go Overseas, a City Struggles to Reinvent Itself," *USA Today*, March 21, 2004.

Peralte C. Paul, "Grill Maker to Close Plant," *Atlanta Journal-Constitution*, November 18, 2004.

Jennifer Reingold, "Into Thin Air," Fastcompany.com, April 2004. www.fastcompany.com/magazine/81/offshore.html.

Loren Steffy, "We Have Seen the Job-Taking Enemy, and 'They' Are Us," *Houston Chronicle*, June 13, 2004.

Kelly Yamanouchi, "Agents Along for the Ride," *Denver Post*, September 18, 2006.

Web Sites

Economics (www.mcwdn.org/ECONOMICS/EconMain.html). A site that offers good, clear explanations of economics, money, jobs, and trade.

PBS, The Outsourcing Debate (www.pbs.org/now/politics/outsourcedebate.html). A brief summary of some of the facts and issues about outsourcing. Includes links to other sites with further information.

Show Us the Jobs, Meet 51 Faces 51 Stories
(www.showusthejobs.com/51stories/).
Includes links to personal stories of displaced
workers. Many lost their jobs because of outsourcing.

Index

Picture Credits

Cover photo: © Harry Maynard/zefa/CORBIS
Maury Aaseng, 14, 17, 23
Associated Press, 5, 10, 21, 24, 28, 29, 43, 46, 52, 53
Peter Bauermeister/Bloomberg News/Landov, 39
© Tibor Bognar/CORBIS, 8
Sherwin Crasto/Reuters/Landov, 15
© David De La Paz/epa/CORBIS, 37
© Dinodia Images/Alamy, 35
Jupiterimages Unlimited/Ablestock, 25
Jupiterimages Unlimited/Comstock, 6, 9, 18
Jupiterimages Unlimited/Thinkstock, 12
© Kamal Kishore/Reuters/CORBIS, 33
© Kim Kulish/CORBIS, 47
© Danny Lehman/CORBIS, 32
Joe Marquette/Bloomberg News/Landov, 46
Newhouse News Service/Landov, 48
Punit Paranjpe/Reuters/Landov, 40
© Christopher Smith/CORBIS, 51
Matthew Staver/Bloomberg News/Landov, 44

About the Author

Stephen Currie has written many books and educational materials for children and young adults. His books include subjects ranging from pianos to Wild West shows and from exploration to math. He lives in New York State with his family.